HANDFEEDING
BABY BIRDS

CONTENTS

Frontis: Baby hand-fed cockatiel. Photo by John Rammel.

Cover photos by Dr. Herbert R. Axelrod.

Front endpapers: Mother budgerigar and her brood. Photo by Harry V. Lacey.

Back endpapers: Pekin robins, also called Pekin nightingales, *Leiothrix lutea.* Photo by Harry V. Lacey.

ISBN 0-87666-992-5

Distributed in the UNITED STATES by T.F.H. Publications, Inc., 211 West Sylvania Avenue, Neptune City, NJ 07753; in CANADA by H & L Pet Supplies Inc., 27 Kingston Crescent, Kitchener, Ontario N2B 2T6; Rolf C. Hagen Ltd., 3225 Sartelon Street, Montreal 382 Quebec; in ENGLAND by T.F.H. Publications Limited, 4 Kier Park, Ascot, Berkshire SL5 7DS; in AUSTRALIA AND THE SOUTH PACIFIC by T.F.H. (Australia) Pty. Ltd., Box 149, Brookvale 2100 N.S.W., Australia; in NEW ZEALAND by Ross Haines & Son, Ltd., 18 Monmouth Street, Grey Lynn, Auckland 2 New Zealand; in SINGAPORE AND MALAYSIA by MPH Distributors Pte., 71-77 Stamford Road, Singapore 0617; in the PHILIPPINES by Bio-Research, 5 Lippay Street, San Lorenzo Village, Makati, Rizal; in SOUTH AFRICA by Multipet Pty. Ltd., 30 Turners Avenue, Durban 4001. Published by T.F.H. Publications Inc., Ltd., the British Crown Colony of Hong Kong. THIS IS THE 1983 EDITION.

HANDFEEDING
BABY BIRDS

JO COOPER

Raising a baby bird by hand demands patience and a knowledge of the differences between various birds. Obviously there is a difference in the needs of a psittacine bird like the day-old dusky lorikeet shown at left (photo by Dale Thompson) and the baby society finches shown below (photo by Mervin F. Roberts).

Preface

Hand raising a baby bird is an art. Yet Ethel Meyer, well known by aviculturists in not only the United States but also in Canada, Australia and Europe, says, "I've taught men with huge strong hands as well as children how to hand raise birds. It's all in knowing how."

Cathy Cunningham, a lovely lady who raises baby birds for the Los Angeles Zoo, told me, "I don't think you can actually teach someone to hand feed. To be honest with you, I think it's something you have to have a knack for, but maybe you can guide them along the right lines."

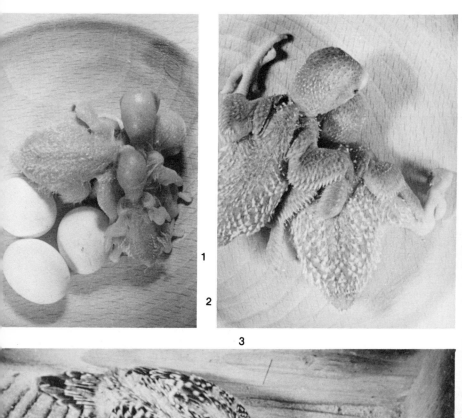

1

2

3

8

That's what this book is . . . just a set of guide lines. Not only do different species of birds need to be treated differently, but each individual bird develops at his own speed and must be handled accordingly.

I am primarily a writer, but the past few years I have also become a bird raiser and, as an apt pupil of Mrs. Meyer, have successfully hand raised finches, canaries and cockatiels.

Ralph Cooper, D.V.M., is a well known veterinarian who specializes in avian diseases at the State of California Laboratory in San Gabriel, California. He also lectures at avicultural and veterinary conventions throughout the United States. His help and advice is greatly appreciated.

Progression in the development of budgerigars bred domestically and raised by their parents: 1. One baby at the age of two days and two babies at the age of six days, shown with unhatched eggs. 2. Fifteen-day-old and seventeen-day-old (with head partially obscured) budgies. 3. Baby budgies at twenty-six days out of the egg. 4. A thirty-day-old baby.

4

Whether the bird to be hand fed is a comparatively inexpensive species like the star finch shown at left or a relatively scarcer and more costly bird like the black-capped lory (below), hand feeding can be a valuable skill. Photos: left, G. Ebben; below; Dr. Herbert R. Axelrod.

Why?

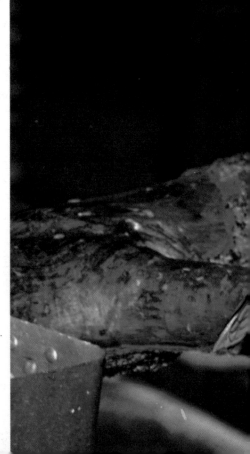

Hand feeding a bird is a chore that takes a lot of time and patience, so some people say, "Why bother?" Most of us smile and shrug, "It's not for the money." Mainly it's because a baby bird is a little living creature struggling to survive. In the wild, if a parent bird pushes a baby out of the nest or decides to abandon it in the nest, it dies.

You may want to hand feed because you've had experience with a certain pair of birds that lay eggs, hatch them and then abandon the babies. Or you may have a pair of rare birds that don't like to reproduce in captivity. If you get fertile eggs from these expensive birds you may want to incubate them and hand raise them if you've had bad luck with the parents raising the babies before.

People who are raising birds just for profit may take the babies out of the nest to get a double clutch. For instance, if you're raising lutino and albino ringneck parakeets, you could get eight babies a year instead of four. The scarlet macaws that Cathy Cunningham has now were feather-picked by their parents, so the zoo took them out of the nest when they were six weeks old.

You may just want to pull a baby bird out of the nest and hand feed it so you'll have a tame bird. Tame birds are not only worth more money, they are a greater pleasure to their owner.

The first bird in our collection was an albino cockatiel that Mrs. Meyer started hand feeding and gave to me as a present. "Toby" is now three years old and a great family favorite. He acts as "watch dog," setting up a screeching whenever we have a visitor. We occasionally let him out of his cage, and he likes to run along the back of our couch. He also has a ball turning pages of a paperback book or the TV guide and chattering away almost like a person mumbling. Stephen lets him nibble at his hair and Ralph lets him ride around the house on his shoulder. Cockatiels make good pets and are not too hard to train to talk. Toby says "pretty bird, pretty bird" quite plainly when he feels like it. Since he has seniority over all the other birds in the house, I'm afraid he's a bit cocky.

Quite often the parent birds will knock a baby out of the nest. Sometimes it's an accident, as when the baby gets caught on the parent's foot, but sometimes it is with good reason. The parents know something is seriously wrong with the baby and it is going to die. I mention this because you must be prepared that some of the babies you try to hand feed will die, but you know for sure they'll die if no one feeds them. Maybe with your help they can overcome what trouble they have, but maybe not.

Sometimes birds are hand fed to keep a species of birds from becoming extinct. For instance, the nene goose found in Hawaii got down to just a few pair. With the help of concerned aviculturists in the United States, they've raised enough to return them to their normal habitat in Hawaii.

"Until proper breeding requirements are discovered," Richard Rundel, Curator of Birds, Los Angeles Zoo, said, "exotic bird breeding is on a very sporadic and rarely self-sustaining basis." Thus many zoos and some private bird farms raise eggs in incubators and/or hand feed babies to help a species along that's having trouble.

There are many reasons why you might want to feed a baby bird. If you are really ready to spend the time, I'll try to help you get on the right track.

This six-week-old nene goose, one of the species whose numbers are being increased by dedicated aviculturists, was raised at the Los Angeles Zoo. Photo by Dorthy Petrulla.

Lories and lorikeets (Forsten's lorikeet, *Trichoglossus haematodus forsteni,* at right, blue-crowned lory, *Vini australis,* below) have longer weaning periods and a longer post-weaning time before they become completely independent than smaller psittacines such as the budgerigar but much shorter periods than the truly large psittacines like cockatoos and macaws. Photos by San Diego Zoo.

When To Hand Feed A Bird

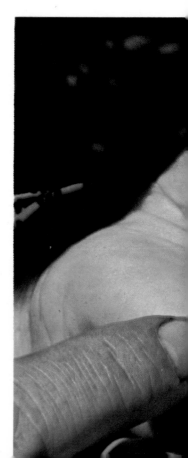

When should you hand feed a bird?

First of all, if the parent birds are not feeding it. Most breeders check the babies before dusk to be sure the crops are full. Some only check once in a while so as not to disturb the nest box. Occasionally you will find a baby bird out of the nest. You can try putting him back in, but watch carefully because if it was a deliberate eviction, he'll get dumped again soon.

You should hand feed a bird if you want a tame bird. It is necessary to take him out of the nest within a week of when he would normally come out. This varies with each species. A Lady Gouldian finch, for instance, you could take out about six days after he's hatched. Psittacines of course can be older.

1. These hungry baby canaries were hatched by the female parent shown (2) incubating the eggs. Photos by Harry V. Lacey.

You may want to hand feed the first clutch of new breeders. You have to watch young, inexperienced breeders. I had a pair of canaries who let me raise their first two clutches (seven birds) before they finally decided to feed all those little mouths themselves. We still have "Georgie," my first hand raised canary, a lovely singing male who is very tame two years later.

Sometimes finches will feed their young as long as they are in the nest box, but as soon as they are old enough to fly out, they abandon the runt. Watch for one lonely bird on the floor of your aviary who is not strong enough to fly up to the parent birds and beg for food. He may need just a few supplemental feedings to get him strong enough to compete with his siblings. If you have finches that aren't raising their young, a good thing to try before you go to the hand raising route is to put either the eggs or the babies under society finches. These dear little birds will become foster-parents to all kinds of Australian finches. Just be sure to remove their own eggs or babies.

COMPARATIVE NESTING PERIODS

	Incubation Period	Fledging Age	Weaning Period	Age at Independence
Budgerigar	18 days	5 weeks	1 week	6 weeks
Cockatiel	18-21 days	5 weeks	2 weeks	7 weeks
Love birds	22-25 days	6-7 weeks	2 weeks	8-9 weeks
Grass parakeets	18 days	5 weeks	2 weeks	7 weeks
Ringneck parakeets	18 days	5 weeks	4-5 weeks	9-10 weeks
Typical parrots	28 days	8 weeks (longer for African Grey)	5-6 weeks	13-14 weeks
Lories and lorikeets	28 days	4-5 weeks	4 weeks	8-9 weeks
Cockatoos	28 days	8 weeks	5-6 weeks	13-14 weeks
Macaws	28 days	12-13 weeks	8-10 weeks	20-23 weeks
Finches	11-13 days	2-2½ weeks	2½ weeks	4½-5 weeks

No matter what type of bird you're dealing with, don't attempt a hand feeding program unless you're able to see it through to completion, and don't attempt it with birds being fed normally by their parents. Left: Indian ringneck parakeets, *Psittacula krameri manillensis,* photo by Dale Thompson; below, mother canary and babies.

When You Should Not Hand Feed A Bird

Don't start to hand feed a baby bird if you are not going to be able to continue until it is weaned. This time varies with species as well as each individual bird, but you must figure a possibility of five to six weeks for a finch or up to ten weeks or more if it's a macaw. You will need to be home every two hours at first and then at least three times a day, so check your calendar and plan your time first. If you have a special three-day weekend trip planned away from home, you may have a hard time finding a "bird sitter" who can handle the hand feeding process.

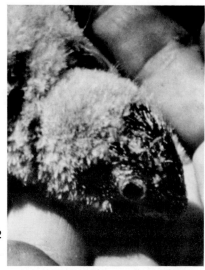

1

2

3

Don't hand feed the babies if the parent birds are doing a good job on their own. It's like a breast-fed baby: the mother's formula is much healthier than any we can concoct.

Dale Thompson, Director, Behavioral Studies of Birds and Animals, Newhall, California, and the past Asssociate Curator of Birds, Los Angeles Zoo, says, "Don't pull eggs unless you have to. Whenever possible let the adults raise their young. Undoubtedly, you'll have a better bird."

Do not be tempted to bring wild birds into your house to raise ... especially if you have any exotic birds in your home. Neighbor children are apt to deliver wild birds that have dropped out of the nest to the "bird lady" on the block because they know you know how to handle birds. Almost all wild birds carry parasites. They may also carry bird diseases such as Newcastle, salmonella and psittacosis that could kill your pet bird or endanger your own health. Contact your local zoo or veterinarian. In some areas there are individuals who have a house full of nothing but wild birds. Let them take the wild baby. It's against the law in most states to keep a wild bird as a pet, so even if you did raise it, you'd have to let it go again and it might not make it outside on its own without proper training.

Often it is necessary to remove babies from their parents to prevent the babies from being killed by the parents or from dying of neglect if the parents refuse to care for them. Shown here are three stages in the growth of a baby scaly-breasted lorikeet. 1. The baby at four-days of age. 2. Closeup of the head of the same bird at two weeks of age. 3. The bird at the age of one month. Photos by Dale Thompson at Los Angeles Zoo.

1. Closeup of a newly hatched scaly-breasted lorikeet, *Trichoglossus chlorolepidotus.* 2. The same bird at an age of about 1½ months. 3. Adult scaly-breasted lorikeets. Photos: 1 and 2 by San Diego Zoo; 3 by Dale Thompson.

Baby society finches in the nest prepared for them by their parents. Photo by Mervin F. Roberts. *Below:* a trayful of eggs of different bird species at the Los Angeles Zoo. Photo by Dale Thompson.

Nest Boxes

The first thing you need when you do decide to feed a bird by hand is a place to keep him. You are taking him from under his mama's body in a nest she made especially for him. Your nest will have to be different. It must be warm and comfortable and not too hard for you to clean. Baby birds can become very messy without a mama to clean up after their waste.

Until the baby gets its pin feathers you must keep it in a brooder at about 92-94 degrees Fahrenheit. I have made a make-shift brooder of the standard shoe box variety for

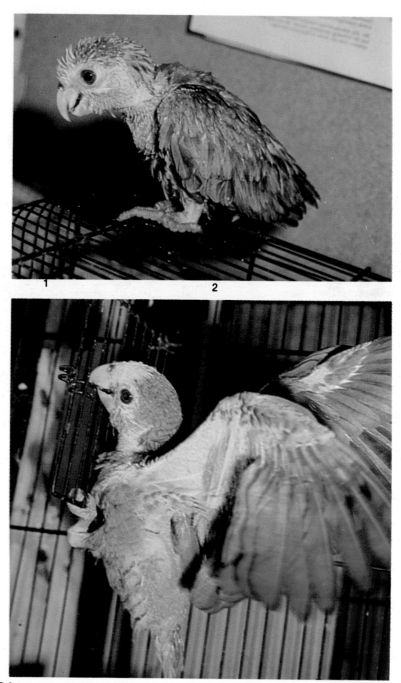

3

Hand feeding allows for the propagation of species that are rarely bred in captivity; in some cases, aviculturists are able to do very good work in continuing to perpetuate species that happen to be endangered in their native areas. Shown here are African and Asiatic parrot species bred and raised in captivity. 1. and 2. A young yellow-faced African parrot, *Poicephalus flavifrons,* at two stages in its development. 3. Two different Asiatic species (a 15-day-old blue-crowned hanging parrot, *Loriculus galgalus,* the smaller bird, and a 36-day-old vernal hanging parrot, *Loriculus vernalis).* Photos: 1 and 2 by Dale Thompson; 3 by San Diego Zoo.

finches and canaries. It has a 15-watt light bulb in one end and a burlap-covered margarine carton in the other. I put a light-weight dish towel over the top. We have also used an old fish tank, without the water of course, but utilizing the light and heater.

After the bird begins to feather you can reduce the heat to about 88 degrees. When fully feathered, move it into a cage and only cover him at night. Be extra careful to avoid drafts from air conditioners, as you do with your adult birds.

Zoos and farms use commercial incubators and brooders. Inside the brooder you need a special container for the baby. Depending entirely on the size and species of bird you have, you may use a plastic margarine container lined with burlap.

Eleanor Coolie, a southern California bird raiser, says, "When they're little I take a strawberry basket and put an inexpensive wash rag in it with a rubber band around the top to hold it in place. Then as they grow I change to cardboard boxes and sometimes I use flannelette diapers or old cut up sheet blankets." You can wash these little cloths just like diapers.

Mrs. Meyers often puts a baby bird in a half-gallon plastic ice cream carton about one-third filled with wood shavings which are carefully topped with a paper towel. She puts the container on top of her gas stove so that the heat from the pilot light keeps the birds warm. Dr. Cooper says the gas fumes are not particularly good for the bird, but this is certainly a good way to remind yourself you have a baby to feed every few hours. Mrs. Meyer has been successfully hand raising birds for eighteen years.

The use of wood chips under baby birds is debatable. Some bird fanciers use them because they are absorbent and keep the babies clean. Dr. Cooper and other veterinarians cry out in alarm because they have opened too many dead birds and found a crop full of tiny wood shavings.

Cathy Cunningham, the L.A. Zoo baby raiser, said, "I

really liked wood chips because their feet don't get dirty and the underneath part where the navel is can get infected so easily if it isn't kept clean. But I almost lost a two-week-old umbrella cockatoo once. I had problems the thirteenth and fourteenth days with slow digestion—sour crop—and on the fifteenth day I had to go in with a syringe and remove the food from his crop and I came out with a piece of wood shaving. Now I use paper towel. They feed on that, too, but it doesn't break off. If they can get an edge of it and it feels right, they'll feed on it. "Buttons," a little umbrella cockatoo I raised for Jack Kelly, even fed on an unused light socket. He really thought his mother was weird looking."

What you really need as an alternate nest box is a soft and warm container a little larger than the bird and with some type of material to give him support. Facial tissue can be too slippery. Remember never to place a baby bird's feet on a slippery table or you can cause spraddle leg.

Spraddle leg is a common defect in birds. Instead of the legs being parallel, they are spread apart in an obtuse angle. Besides the grotesque appearance, the poor bird is unable to walk, perch or even reach the seed or water dish.

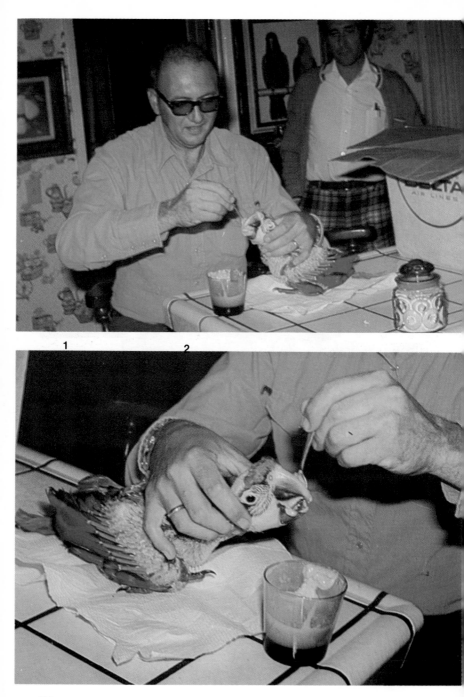

1   2

3

Dick Topper of Gilroy, California, reputed to possess one of the best collections of Australian psittacine birds in the United States, is shown here tending to the hand feeding of a Catalina macaw. 1. Dick feeding the macaw from a spoon. 2. Closeup of the spoon-feeding operation; notice how the head of the bird is supported as it eats. 3. Even at its obviously young age, the macaw is able to perch safely on its owner's arm. (The Catalina macaw is a hybrid between the scarlet macaw and the blue and gold macaw.) Photos by Dale Thompson.

The baby cockatiels shown at left and below thrived on the formula provided them by their breeder (note the stuffed crops of the birds at left). It was messy, but they loved it. Photos by John Rammel.

What To Feed

There are as many formulas as there are birds, so I will just give you one for finches, canaries and small birds and also the 1-2-3 step formula for psittacines.

Remember that the mother bird regurgitates the food and carefully places it in the babies' beaks. You and I can't do this, so we make do the best we can with a good substitute.

The formula should be runny. You do NOT ever feed baby birds water alone. The liquid they get will be in the formula. Of course, the more liquid it is the bigger the mess you'll make. I haven't invented a bird bib yet, so you will

get it all over the bird. "Toby" was my first experience hand raising anything, and I made such a mess of him; the feathers near his crop became so matted that Mrs. Meyer took him home and bathed him for me.

The formula must be at the right temperature. You can check it just like a baby bottle by placing a little on the inside of your wrist. It should be warm, not too hot, and you must not let it get cold during the feeding. I found an old pink baby dish at a garage sale, the kind that you can put hot water in, and it's perfect for heating formula. Many people use a single egg poacher pan with the formula in a small ceramic bird seed dish sitting in the hot water.

FINCH AND/OR CANARY FORMULA

First day or two:	¼ cup water
	2 teaspoons Instant Cream of Wheat*
	Cook and stir constantly for about 30 seconds, just until it starts to thicken.
	Place in baby dish (or container) and while it is cooling to the correct temperature wash your pan and spoon immediately. (They clean easily at this point, but if they dry you are scouring later.)
Then add:	pinch of ground hulled millet (you can get hulled millet in health stores, put handful in blender to grind and store in covered plastic container)
	sprinkle of strained hardboiled egg (I push it through a coarse tea strainer, or you could grate it)
And once a day:	sprinkle of ground cuttlebone tiny cut up greens

* If you are away from the stove or haven't the time to cook Cream of Wheat each time, you can substitute Gerber's Mixed Cereal mixed with hot water, but the cooked cereal seems to be much better for the tiny or sickly little birds.

PSITTACINE FORMULAS

Formula 1:
 ½ cup boiling water
 1 tblsp. Wheathearts (not instant)
 cook 3 to 5 minutes
 Add: 1 egg yolk
     1 heaping teaspoon powdered milk
     1 tsp. honey
     ½ jar oatmeal with applesauce and bananas (baby food)
     ¼ tsp. ground cuttlebone

Formula 2:
 2½ cups boiling water
 2 tsp. corn oil
 dash salt
 ½ cup Wheathearts
 cook 3 to 5 minutes
 Add: ½ cup powdered milk
     1 jar oatmeal with applesauce and bananas
     1 tblsp. honey
     ⅓ cup sunflower meal
     ¼ tsp. ground cuttlebone

Formula 3:
 6 cups boiling water
 1 cup Quick Oatmeal
 ½ cup Wheathearts
 1 tblsp. corn oil
 ½ tsp. salt
 cook 3 to 5 minutes
 Add: ½ jar strained peas
     ½ jar strained spinach
     ½ jar strained carrots
     1 cup powdered milk
     2 cups sunflower meal
     ½ tblsp. ground cuttlebone

If formulas get lumpy, beat with egg beater while cooking. Refrigerate in tightly covered plastic containers and reheat for each feeding.

1

2

3

These psittacine formulas are fine for budgerigars, cockatiels, love birds, parakeets, parrots, lories and lorikeets, cockatoos or macaws. You want to change the birds from one formula to the next gradually. You don't stop Formula 1 one day and start Formula 2 the next. Change formulas when it is going through their system too fast or their weight gain is too slow. This varies with each species and individual birds. Normally when you are up to the stage where you are feeding the bird every three hours instead of two, and every time you go to feed him the crop is empty, it's time to change. With a severe macaw it was only seven days. With an umbrella cockatoo it was about fourteen days.

When you change to the next formula mix ⅔ of the old with ⅓ of the new for a day or two, then half and half, then ⅔ new, then all new.

If you have a baby bird you want to feed, you have probably been feeding its parents. Therefore, you know the correct diet the bird should have as an adult. Work with this in mind when you make the baby's formula. Lories, for instance, like more fruit, so you add more applesauce. Cockatiels may like ground sunflower seeds. Carnivorous birds, such as the roadrunner, may require cut up mice and crickets. The main thing is to grind up or cut up their regular diet small enough for a baby bird to digest it.

Different birds will of course have varying feeding formula requirements. The three birds shown (1. chattering lory; 2. Anna's hummingbird; 3. baby mynah birds) represent three widely disparate families and need different feeding regimens. (Photo 1 by Vogelpark Walsrode, 2 by Dale Thompson, 3 by Rene Halbraken.)

Feeding a Germain peacock pheasant with a syringe. Photo by Dale Thompson. *Below:* "Buttons," a 6-week-old umbrella cockatoo owned by Jack Kelly, being fed by Tami Cunningham. Photo by the author.

How?

Now you have the baby bird in a comfortable container, you've mixed up the proper formula and have checked its temperature. How do you get it into the bird? The first time with each bird is difficult, and if you've never hand fed before, your first time may be frustrating for both you and the bird.

First, how do you hold the bird? Again, this differs with species and size of bird, but in all cases you must have a firm hold, with special care to support the head (just like you do a human baby) and hold it firmly so it doesn't fall. Mrs. Meyer lays small finches on their backs when she

starts feeding them. Cathy Cunningham always feeds the birds with them standing upright, but she is usually handling psittacines or larger birds. She holds the bird in her hand and sits on the floor or the bed. "A lot of people feed them at the kitchen table," she explained, "but they have to be very careful because the bird is quick and can wiggle out of your hand. If it drops from the table to the floor it may be hurt badly." She usually sits on the floor near her coffee table.

I usually feed at the kitchen table. With a new bird I might put a soft towel on the table in case it slips out of my hand. You soon learn that your baby bird is just like a real baby. You can't turn your back or leave them unattended, or they'll roll off the table. Little birds grow so fast that you never know when one who has always stood perfectly still in one place is suddenly old enough to scoot the entire width of the table or even make a little flying leap into the air. Another safeguard I always take when feeding babies is to lock our dog in another room. A baby bird just learning to fly, or one too young to fly, is just too much of a temptation for most dogs.

Experiment and find what is most comfortable for you and your bird. The first day or so will be the only difficult time. After the bird learns you are supplying what he wants most—food—he will cooperate with an open beak and flapping wings.

The type of utensil you use depends on the size of the bird and, of course, on what you have available. For a tiny finch you can start with the flat end of a toothpick, an artist's brush, a small 3 cc syringe or, as I much prefer, a 3" piece of 5/16" plastic tubing with the end cut off on a slant. This is pliable, yet firm enough to pry open the tiny beak. You can also use an eyedropper to feed little birds.

Most people feed with a syringe, a 3 cc for small birds and a 10 cc for cockatiels or larger birds. Of course you do not use the needle. You may have to cut off the opening with scissors to get the formula through. Place the formula in the large end and push it through slowly, just into the beak, and without air bubbles if possible.

If you get air in the crop, you should burp your baby. This is accomplished by the experts by gently massaging the crop from the base upward. Mrs. Meyer does it beautifully with even the tiniest finches, but I've not been as successful. Every time I try to pry the beak open with a toothpick for the burp to get out, it seems like I let more air in. Cockatiels especially need burping, but they are a little more cooperative.

Mrs. Towne, well known cockatiel raiser in southern California, says, "The cockatiels seem to swallow more air, and a person who doesn't know how to hand feed a bird will feed more air. You don't rub it, you just get at the base of the crop and work the bubble up through the throat and all of a sudden you'll hear it burp."

The only problem with using a syringe is that if the bird isn't eating and you aren't keyed to look for this or know what to look for, then the food could go into the windpipe by mistake. I've done this with tiny Lady Gouldian babies and had them shudder and die in my hand (and I cried, but I learned and did better the next time). Be firm but gentle and just put it in their beaks. Let the experts put things directly into or take things out of the crop.

Almost all cockatiels are fed with a syringe. Psittacines can be started with a syringe but are soon changed over to spoons that are shaped into a scoop. Cathy Cunningham uses the syringe to measure the amount fed on the spoon and says, "You want to use the spoon with a jerky, in and out action, as much like the parent's beak moving in and out as possible."

Some people use a doser (a metal syringe used for cows), a battery filler or a baster (a plastic tube with a bulb at one end) instead of a syringe, but no matter what you use, you'll have a hard time at first convincing the baby he should open his beak for you. You can tap it on the side or on the top like the parent bird does, but tiny, frightened, starving baby birds are not likely to understand what you are trying to do at first. Pry his beak open with the tube feeder or syringe. Be gentle but firm. It's usually easier from the side. After a day or two they'll open their beaks and respond to you as if you were a mother bird.

You may *feel* like a mama bird when it seems that every time you turn around it's time to feed again, but once you get the knack of it, it will only take a few minutes of your time. However, spend a little extra time because the difference between successful and unsuccessful hand feeders is T.L.C. (Tender Loving Care)!

Mrs. Meyer, Cathy Cunningham and several other experts I've observed all have one thing in common. They care! They not only feed the bird, they give it love, lots of gentle handling and an abundance of conversation and soothing tones to help it through a trying time. These frightened, lonely baby birds need extra attention if they are to survive without their parent bird's care.

If you are going to feed a psittacine, you'd best first trim its beak and nails. You may get hurt worse by a scratch from the feet than by a bite when it's a baby. Their natural instinct is to roll over and get you with their feet, and they are quick. You can get out of the way of their beak faster than out of the way of their feet.

The Cunninghams raised five beautiful scarlet macaws from six-week-old babies. They were being badly feather-picked by their parents in the Los Angeles Zoo. Before Cathy could get their nails trimmed, one of them scratched her arm quite badly. By the time they were fourteen weeks old, her nine-year-old son, David, and a twelve-year-old girl, Tami, could cradle them in their arms like babies.

Children are great with birds and it's a good hobby for them. My thirteen-year-old son, Stephen, helps immeasurably in the care and raising of our birds. When he was younger (and shorter) it was much easier for him to change the paper, etc. in our walk-in aviary in the house, because he could stand up straight without hitting his head on the perches. Small hands are not quite as much of a threat in a small cage as a large hand that takes up half the bird's space. It's a good way for children to earn a little more allowance and give you a day off once in a while.

Check your baby every two hours or so, but do not feed him again until his crop is empty. Also be sure he assimilates what you feed him. If not, it may mean he has crop mold, needs a diet change, is cold or is just sick.

The amount you feed corresponds directly with the size of your bird's crop. A small finch may only need half a teaspoon, but a psittacine may need four ounces. It is better to feed a little bit every few hours than to overfeed.

These parent budgies are taking good care of their babies, but not all birds that breed in captivity take care of their young. In some cases, luckily, a bird that fails to fulfill its parental duties the first time it is mated performs satisfactorily with later clutches. Photo by Harry V. Lacey.

Regardless of the species of bird being fed or the reason for which it is being fed (left, orange weaver having vitamin drops administered to it; below, the author's first hand fed pet bird, an albino cockatiel, being fed with a syringe), cleanliness of the feeding instruments is very important. Photos by Louise Van der Meid and the author.

Cleanliness

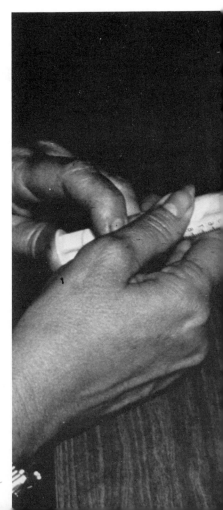

This may sound like I'm reminding you to wash dishes after dinner, but really, it is extremely important when you raise birds that you clean up *immediately*. As I mentioned earlier, cereal formulas are sticky and just like glue if you allow them to dry. If you do not rinse out your utensils immediately after each use, particles may remain to promote bacterial or fungal infections.

Cleaning immediately following feeding also saves you time. I want you to enjoy hand feeding and have time to play with your bird and enjoy him, not spend all your time with a scouring pad.

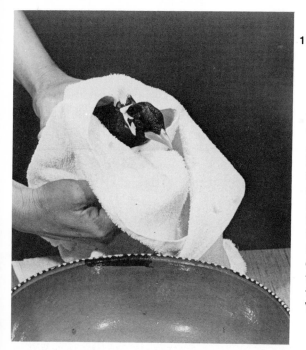

1. Using a fluffy bath towel to dry off a mynah bird. 2. A mynah bird bathing itself; note the vigorous splashing action. 3. One canary is already in the bath and another is about to join him. Birds enjoy bathing, but you have to make sure that a warm, draft-free area is provided for them to dry off in after the bath. Photos by Harry V. Lacey.

And don't forget your hands. Be sure to scrub up before each feeding. Dr. Cooper says, "The young birds are even more susceptible to diseases than adult birds. They can easily get crop mold or worse if you don't wash your hands well before feeding."

Even more important than cleaning the utensils and your hands is cleaning the bird. No matter how careful you are, you will get formula on the bird. Take a soft wash rag or piece of wet cotton and clean the bird right away. He won't like it, but children don't either and they both survive.

After your bird is fully feathered you can bathe it, but be sure you get it thoroughly dry. The Cunninghams bathed their macaws from the time they were feathered every three or four days. They put them in the bath tub with the water deep enough so that when they stood up in it their underside was in the water. They used lukewarm water, of course. Then they dried them with a hair dryer.

3

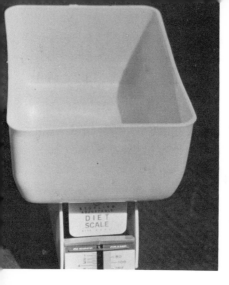

Given proper nourishment, baby birds grow quickly; for keeping track of their development, a scale that accurately measures small weights will come in handy. Photo by the author. *Below:* a day-old Germain peacock pheasant. Photo by Dale Thompson.

Records

Keep records. It is very important, especially if you are hand feeding several different kinds of birds at a time. It's like a hospital with different kinds of medication. You need to know exactly how much you administered, to whom and at what time. You need to keep track of the weight. If your baby doesn't gain anything in a two-day period, you know you have a problem. You must be sure it is passing its droppings properly. You'll know because no mama bird is there to clean up after him.

Even if your baby dies, keep the records. Next time you need to try, you'll have a head start because you'll know exactly what you did.

A nightingale mother feeding her hungry youngsters. Photo by John Warham. *Below:* In the wild, even nocturnal species like owls don't feed their young at night. Human foster parents, however, should provide nighttime feedings. Photo by Robert J. Higgins.

Night Feeding

Experts disagree about whether it is necessary to hand feed birds at night or not. Veterinarians and scientists insist that all birds hibernate in total darkness and that parent birds do not feed their young at night. But most of the successful hand feeders I interviewed said they always feed at night, every two hours, the first two or three days they have a new bird.

Birds hatched in an incubator are fed at night for about two weeks. Maybe it's the light from the heater that wakes

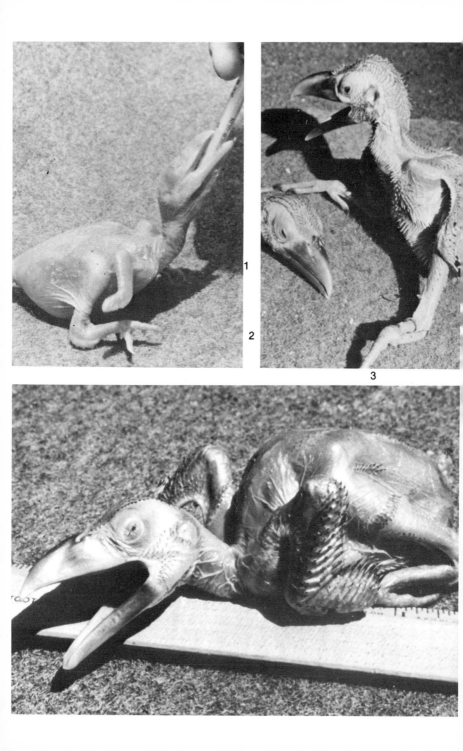

them up and starts their digestive systems working, maybe it's just because what we feed them is not as satisfying as that fed by the parent bird, but I recommend hand feeding every two hours around the clock until the bird is eating well and has gained weight.

Try to weigh your bird at least every other day. You can permanently attach a plastic dish to a postage scale or any scale that has ten-gram divisions.

Stages in the development of the pale-mandibled aracari, an altricial bird raised at the Los Angeles Zoo. 1. one week old; 2. 29 days old; 3. being measured at the age of 26 days; 4. adult. Photos by Dale Thompson.

4

A down-covered infant cockatiel can rapidly develop into an alert and perpetually hungry youngster like the pin-feathered baby cockatiels below. But regardless of the speed of their development, individual birds differ in their willingness to be weaned away from the hand-feeding regimen. Photos by Dr. Gerald R. Allen.

Weaning

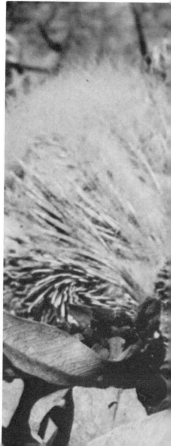

As soon as your baby bird is fully feathered and moved out of the brooder, his cage floor should have seed and gravel on it. Birds have a natural pecking habit, and you want the right food for them.

It's easier if you have more than one baby because one is always brighter than the rest and, once they see him pecking, they'll copy. When I raised "Georgie" the canary, I placed another small cage with an adult canary in it beside Georgie's cage on my kitchen table so he could watch. The old adage "monkey see, monkey do" works with birds as well.

With the Lady Gouldians and canaries I started weaning at about five to six weeks. They were digesting ground millet in their formula, and then I'd dip the end of the

Here a mother canary seems to be scolding one of her youngsters for its greedy demands for food. Remember that baby birds that you undertake to hand feed will make as large a demand for your attention and care as they'd make on their mother. Photo by Lilo Hess, Three Lions.

feeding tube or syringe with formula on it into a little pile of whole hulled millet . . . just one seed at a time. It will stick to the moist formula until you get it up to the beak. Soon they'll be eating about six seeds a feeding.

"Toby," my cockatiel, tricked me into hand feeding him for about three months because I didn't know any better. As you saw on the chart, I should have been free in about five to six weeks. Some birds are very independent and, as soon as they can, will eat by themselves and have little to do with you. Others, like shy children grasping at your apron strings, refuse anything except what you put in their mouths. Then you need to let them get hungry. Don't starve them. Always be sure they have a full crop at night, but when you think they are old enough cut down to just one feeding a day and offer a good variety of food for them to eat on their own. Place food on the floor of the cage at first, as they can find it easier there than in a seed dish.

There are other things you must teach your baby at this stage besides just how to eat by himself. For instance, he has no mother bird to teach him that it is more comfortable and a lot healthier to sit on a perch than on the cage floor. You can help this along if you place a small branch in the cage so it makes a ramp from the floor to the first perch. Be sure it is secured properly and has no rough edges. (Remember, I'm talking about a fully feathered, half-grown baby now, not a tiny new one.)

Birds also need exercise. As soon as the psittacines the Cunninghams raise are feathered, they are played with. The children carry them away to their bedroom and play with them as you would a dog or cat.

When your tame birds are old enough to fly or just hop fairly fast, be sure that you learn to close unscreened windows and keep your doors locked. No, the birds aren't smart enough to unlock them, but an unsuspecting soul from outside is liable to open your door and out will fly three months' worth of tame bird.

This week-old white guinea fowl is comparatively much more advanced in development than the canaries shown below. Photo at left by Dale Thompson; photo below by Lilo Hess, Three Lions.

Unusual Birds Hand Raised at the Los Angeles Zoo

(From an interview with Dale Thompson, Director, Behavioral Studies of Birds and Animals, Newhall, California, and past Associate Curator of Birds, Los Angeles Zoo.)

Most hand raised birds are precocial birds; that is, once started on food they can readily feed themselves. Altricial birds, on the other hand, are hatched completely helpless; most are blind and without feathers. This type of bird is seldom hand raised. The bird keepers at the Los Angeles Zoo have raised four different species of altricial birds: the roadrunner *(Geococcyx californianus);* kookaburra *(Dacelo novaguineae);* frogmouth *(Podargus strigoides strigoides);* and pale-mandibled aracari *(Pteroglossus erythropygius),* a kind of toucan.

The roadrunner and kookaburra eggs were incubated in an incubator. Of the first twenty-seven hatched, they lost twenty-six chicks. Some had internal problems, some were just overfed. It was so discouraging they almost gave up. Toward the end they were raising every single one of them.

One of the frogmouth eggs was artificially incubated and hatched, but it's easier if the parent bird raises it at least halfway. It's best to leave the eggs under the parent bird until the last day before it is due to hatch and then place it in an incubator. This gives you a stronger chick and prevents the adults from eating the young.

All of the pale-mandibled aracari chicks were incubated under parent birds, but the pair the Los Angeles Zoo had did not seem to want to know how to rear them. They threw all the newly hatched chicks out of the nest, a harrowing seventeen feet. Surprisingly, the bird keepers were able to rescue a few before they got too cold. It was hard to believe that no internal damage was done.

Two methods were used for brooding the chicks. A non-rocking Lyons incubator with a temperature starting at 95 degrees and dropping five degrees every week or two as needed was one. The other method was to use a heating pad beneath the small nest and keep the internal nest temperature at the above temperatures. The heating pad simulated the brood patch of the adult bird. Plastic strawberry containers were used for nests. At first they used toweling in them, but this was a mistake. They found you must put twigs or natural things that would be in the nest so the baby's feet won't curl. Aracaris take forty-six days to get out of the nest. They are kept in a log-like nest at the zoo.

The main diet for these birds was baby mice, known as "pinkies," cut up and fed with forceps. Later they added soaked dog food, cricket bodies and meal worms. Two pale-mandibled aracaris were raised to adults on baby mice, soft portions of grapes (not the skins) and bananas to keep the moisture and sugar content at a high level. A vitamin powder was added once a day and several cc's of water were given at each feeding. Remember, if you are feeding chunk food such as the mice, you must add water. If you are feeding a cereal formula, no water is needed.

The first day a bird hatches in the incubator it is not fed at all, the second day they feed every hour or two depending on when the crop is empty, then after the first week it's up to every three hours.

There are twelve species of frogmouths found from India to Australia. The tawny frogmouth exhibited at the Los Angeles Zoo is found from southeastern Queensland to New South Wales. When the chick is first hatched it is covered with fine hair-like white feathers that completely cover its eyes. Three weeks later its color has changed and it has the look of an old weather-beaten log; its feather pattern looks like bark. When frightened this bird will freeze into a rigid upright position and appear as a broken tree limb.

(John Tobin and Dale Thompson worked on these projects at the Los Angeles Zoo in 1974 and 1975.)

Zoos have to hand raise a lot of babies because they display for color and appearance rather then perfect breeding conditions. The Los Angeles and San Diego Zoos both have large walk-in aviaries, which means hundreds of strange people are walking through the birds' territories all the time. This is not too conducive to breeding wild birds in captivity. Therefore, it is often necessary to incubate the eggs and hand raise the babies.

Sometimes the climate is not correct. The crimson-rumped toucanet, for instance, raises its young very nicely in southern California except in January, when they figure it's too cold. So every January the zoo keepers know to take the eggs and incubate them, then figure on hand raising the young.

Ringneck parakeets are noted for not raising their young. These birds, originally from India, are often hand raised. Unlike almost all other hand fed birds, these little dickens revert to being nasty and independent after they are weaned. Most hand raised birds remain pets for life, at least to the person who has fed them.

Contrast the pattern of coloration of the week-old tawny frogmouth (1) with that of the same bird as shown at three weeks of age (2) and nine weeks of age (3) and the adult birds (4). Photos by Dale Thompson.

4

Wild birds, whether they're strictly predacious (and potentially dangerous) species like the owl held by the girl at the left or the tiny hummingbird perched on the eyeglasses of noted bird expert Hank Bates below, pose a number of problems for people who want to hand rear them.

Wild Birds

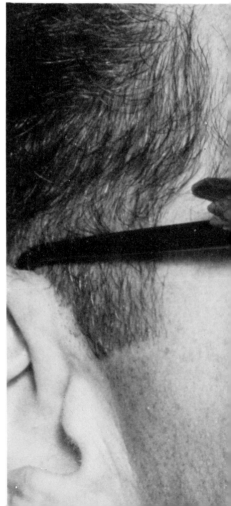

Although I told you earlier NOT to bring wild birds into your home, I realize it's only human nature to want to assist a helpless bird, be it an exotic, expensive psittacine or a tiny sparrow.

For instance, suppose a wild bird hits your clean window. You hear a thud, you see a smudge, maybe a feather is stuck on the glass and you look down into the flower bed below and, sure enough, there is a bird lying there. It may appear lifeless or it might be twitching slightly. Do NOT rush out to him to help. The shock of a human touching him or even coming too close may kill him.

The feeding of adult birds such as these mynah birds by hand is, in addition to being pleasurable in itself, valuable as a means to reinforcing the desirable behavior on the part of the bird, as it allows the owner to offer an immediate reward to the bird for doing the right thing.
1. Feeding an uncaged mynah; 2, 3, 4 show the obvious relish with which a caged mynah takes its hand-fed rations. Photos by Louise Van der Meid.

1

2

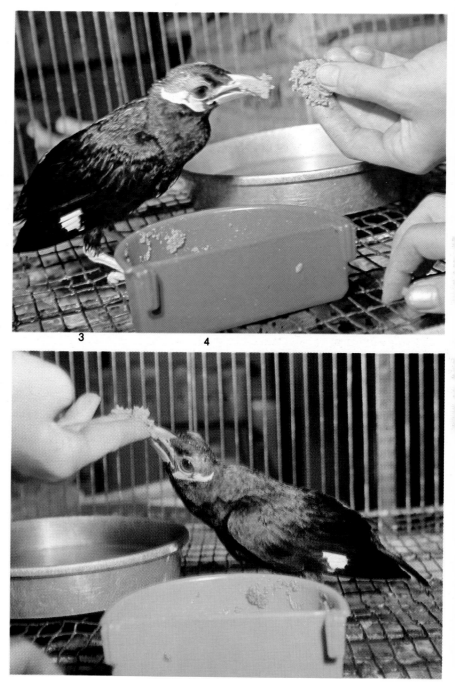

3

4

1

2

The best thing you can do is set up a guard to protect the injured bird from dogs and cats for a short time. Small children are fascinated. Teach them to stand guard but NOT touch. They should stay a good distance away and be quiet so as not to frighten the bird. They must call you if a cat or dog comes into the yard. You will be surprised how many injured birds will seem to "come back to life" if you just leave them alone long enough to get their strength back.

"Mama, a baby bird has fallen out of its nest," is a familiar cry in any household that includes children. Unless you are an expert on wild birds, you may not be able to tell the difference between a baby bird and an adult bird that just happens to be very tiny in size. If there is a possibility that it's an adult, leave it alone for awhile and see if it can get its wind back by itself. If you are sure its a baby—sometimes you can see the nest—then you have a problem. If the nest is accessible you can try to replace the baby in the nest. It's advisable to use a rag or dish towel to handle the bird as some people believe the mother bird will reject an infant that has been handled by a human being. More likely mama rejected it in the first place and will just kick it out of the nest again. If you have no exotic birds in your home and you are determined to try to raise a wild baby, perhaps in your garage or a separate building, place the bird on a towel in a box and then try to follow the instructions given in earlier chapters.

In most states it is against the law to keep wild birds caged, so make it clear to your youngsters at the onset that as soon as the bird can make it on its own it must be set free. If you have rescued a rare species, you can contact your local zoo and they might help or advise you.

1. A roadrunner at the age of one week. 2. The same bird at the age of two weeks. Photos by Dale Thompson.

1

1. Adult thick-billed parrots, *Rhynchopsitta pachyrhyncha pachyrhyncha.* Young birds of this species, rarely bred in captivity, are shown in 2 and 3. In 2 the baby is still young enough to be liberally covered with down; in 3 the baby has progressed considerably in becoming fully feathered, and only a few downy areas remain. Photos: 1, Dr. Matthew M. Vriends; 2 and 3, San Diego Zoo.

2

3

The author's son Stephen and Fred the crow. Photo by the author. Baby birds, whether they're wild birds like crows or pet species like the cockatiel shown below, are completely helpless and must be ministered to constantly.

Raising
A Crow

Once, before we had any exotic birds in the house, we raised a baby crow. Our son Stephen, then just nine years old, had kept careful vigilance with his binoculars of a certain pair of crows who nested every year near the top of a high pine tree nearby.

One morning he came running back to the house with the grave news that one of the baby crows had fallen out of the nest. It was about the size of a robin, seven inches from his beak to his tail. The gray, fuzzy ball huddled on our asphalt driveway. We thought at first it was dead, but then his

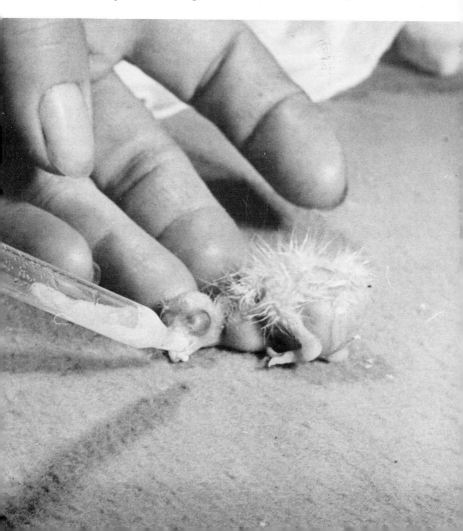

Expensive trainable birds
like macaws are very
suitable candidates for
hand-rearing. 1. Scarlet
macaw, *Ara macao;* 2. Blue
and yellow macaw, *Ara
ararauna.* 3. Tami Cunn-
ingham cradling Captain, a
hand-raised scarlet macaw,
in her arms. Photos: 1, San
Diego Zoo; 2. Dr. Matthew
M. Vriends; 3. Rudd Brown.

beady eyes blinked open. It must have dropped from branch to branch and then into the ivy, as the nest was about 75 feet above us.

We gently put him in an old canary cage and I called Ralph (Dr. Cooper). He told me to forget it, but I didn't want to hurt Stephen, so I thought we could just keep it a day or so until it died.

We phoned Lucille, the "Pasadena Crow Lady," who is an expert with wild birds, and she told us what to feed him. Crows can eat rice, mashed potatoes, scrambled eggs, even avocado and grapes, as well as whole wheat bread, raw meat, cottage cheese, corn, broken up dog biscuits and insects.

"Don't try to force water in it with an eye dropper," she said, "or you'll choke him. You can dip his food in milk or water first when you feed him. He's used to his mother bringing him his food which has been in her mouth, and remember you must put the food way down his throat."

Stephen and I looked at the large red cave of a mouth and wondered if we'd lose a piece of finger, too, if we put them inside. At first we dropped raw hamburger and soaked bread crumbs in from a safe distance above his open mouth, but soon we learned that the beak did not hurt when it closed on our fingers, so we could feed him by pushing a small piece of food way down his throat using our thumb and forefinger like the mother bird had used her beak. When he ate he made a funny noise like "gobble, gobble, gobble." We fed him every two hours until it was dark. He was named Fred, after 'Freddie the Freeloader,' because we had to feed him so much.

Some crows will learn to talk if you repeat the same phrase to them over and over. So every time we fed Fred we'd say "Hello Fred, hello Fred." It's not true that you need to split a crow's tongue in order for him to speak. Fred preferred to say "Caw, caw, caw" loudly whenever we forgot to feed him on time.

76

He grew quickly and we moved him into a turkey cage. We tied some branches in a criss-cross so he could learn to walk and fixed a flower pot saucer with leaves and placed it in one corner for him to sleep in like a nest.

Everyday after school Stephen would take him outside in the sun to play. At first he just hopped around on the grass. Then after a week or two we cut a large dead limb off a tree and put it on the grass so that Fred could hop up onto it and fly down, about a foot or two, to the ground. He climbed all over Stephen and pulled threads out of jeans and tugged at his hair.

Dr. Cooper told us that in four weeks the crow would be able to fly well enough to let him go, but the second week something happened to one wing. It seemed to be sprained . . . I had probably grabbed him too tightly to bring him inside. He loved to play outside and didn't like it when I picked him up because he knew that meant he was going back inside his cage.

After about six weeks he flew all the way from the house to the peach tree, about 15 yards. But he was too scared or too tired to fly back, so Dr. Cooper had to reach up in the tree and carry him back. Each day he flew a little further and was harder to reach.

Stephen wanted to take Fred to school, but the bird lady told him this would frighten Fred too much, so we had a few children at a time come to the house. Finally the teacher came to call. We took Fred outside and for the first time he flew high above the house.

"Hello Fred, hello Fred," we called for him to come back, but some mockingbirds who didn't like Fred being in their territory pecked at him and drove him away. We called after him all the way down the driveway, but he didn't come back.

We worried about him because he hadn't learned to dig for insects and find food outside yet. Some tame crows that are turned loose fly and live in the trees, but come back to a

1

2

It is not possible to imitate exactly the actions of the parent birds in feeding their young, but in many cases we can come fairly close. 1. 4-day-old cockatiel. 2. A baby cockatiel at the age of very close to one month. 3. The male parent cockatiel regurgitating food from its crop and preparing to feed its begging youngster. 4. The young bird taking food from the mouth of its father. Photos by Dr. Gerald R. Allen.

3

4

feeder. Several weeks went by and whenever we'd hear the "caw, caw, caw" of a crow, we'd run outside calling back "Hello Fred, hello Fred" and waving raw liver pieces.

One day we saw five crows sitting high on top of a telephone pole. Four of the birds were together and one smaller, rather scrawny looking one was over to the other side. "Hello Fred, hello Fred," Stephen called. Four crows flew away, but the scrawny one remained. We ran into the house for the liver, but Fred never came down to eat, so we don't know if he survived in the wild or not.

There is no difference in the feeding requirements of different color varieties within a domesticated pet bird species; regardless of the color variety involved, requirements are the same. 1, 2 and 3: three different color varieties of the same species, the popular zebra finch; 4. a mother zebra finch feeding one of her babies. Photos by Harry V. Lacey.

4

1

2

3

One of the greatest satisfactions to be derived from hand raising baby birds is to be able to trace the development of a baby bird from its completely unprepossessing appearance during the first stages of its life right through to its magnificent adulthood. 1. A 4-week-old male red-sided eclectus parrot, *Eclectus roratus polychloros.* 2. Female of same age. 3. Pair of adult red-sided eclectus parrots. 4. Pair of grand eclectus parrots (in both 3 and 4 the female is the bird with the red head and blue breast). Photos: 1 and 2, Vogelpark Walsrode; 3, Dr. Matthew M. Vriends; 4, San Diego Zoo.

Baby birds are subject to danger and disease whether they're brought up by their parents in the wild or human foster parents in captivity, so there is no guarantee of success. *Left:* hand feeding a young quail. Photo by Louise Van der Meid. *Below:* a mother turtle dove and her nestlings. Photo by Eric J. Hosking.

Joys and Heartbreaks

Be prepared for failures. It's heartbreaking, I know, to work so hard with a little bird and feed it every two hours around the clock for several days and have the dear just shudder and die in your hand. I've often wept over little zebra finches that I could replace for less than $3.00. You can't help but think you failed. Most likely there was something wrong with the bird to begin with or the parent wouldn't abandon it.

The most common cause of "crib death" in the hand raising baby birds department is overfeeding. You must let them digest and eliminate what you've fed them. As Dale

1

1. An adult blue-crowned lory, *Vini australis*. 2. A young (but already pin-feathered) blue-crowned lory. 3. Yellow-backed lories, *Lorius garrulus flavopalliata*, at the age of 36 days. Photos by San Diego Zoo.

3

The rewards in terms of satisfaction and a sense of accomplishment are high if you can hand raise any baby bird, but with exotic and comparatively expensive species like the macaw (1) and lorikeet (2) it can make good economic sense as well. Photos by Kerry V. Donnelly.

Thompson said, "The first California roadrunners we tried to hand feed, we lost the first twenty-six birds. The problem was they were overfed. Their crops became impacted. We just tried too hard. Later, when we learned what we were doing, we raised every single one."

Try, try and try again, even if your first attempt fails. If the parent birds have rejected the baby or refuse to sit on the eggs, that baby will die for sure. If you try to hand feed it, at least it has a chance.

The joys of successfully hand raising a bird far outweigh the heartbreaks. You get not only the personal satisfaction, but the joy of a tame pet for years. Nothing breaks the monotony of your daily feeding and care of your birds like reaching into the cage of one of your hand raised babies where you can stroke him or scratch his head, or he jumps on your hand and wants to come outside with you for awhile. They seem to say "thank you" for many years.

It's well worth it, if you have the time and the patience for it. Your hand fed baby will become a member of the family and probably be hard to part with.

Hand raised birds usually become pets. Aviculturists differ in their opinions on whether hand raised birds can be good breeders. Some are and some aren't. It doesn't matter if you breed them with another hand fed bird or not. Dale Thompson says that at the Behavioral Studies of Birds and Animal Farm in Newhall he has a macaw he fed himself. It is in with a wild female, but in the midst of the squawking and yelling during breeding, his tame male will yell out "hello" and then go back to his wild parrot talk.

The percentages are better for breeding, however, if you do not use hand raised birds. Too many end up thinking they're "people" instead of birds.

1

Tracing the development of a clutch of Bengalese (society) finches: 1. Eggs and 2-hour-old hatchlings. 2. The chicks at the age of one week. 3. Considerably much more developed, the babies have their eyes open. 4. Older and more actively squawking for food, the chicks are being fed by their mother. Photos by Mervin F. Roberts.

2

3

4

and each bird is an individual within his species.

Conclusion

As I said in the beginning, this book is just a guideline. The more people I interviewed, the more I realized that I have only scratched the surface of all there is to know about hand raising baby birds. Hopefully this will help you with some basic problems. I highly recommend that, if you have never hand fed before, you contact your local avicultural society and ask who the expert is in your area. Then go and watch how they do it. I have tried to show you with pictures, but there is no way I can cover each species separately, and each bird is an individual within his species, so each one is a little different.

Good luck! You'll need luck and lots of love, but you, too, can be a successful hand raiser.

Even though a baby bird that a person might have hand raised has long since reached the point of having to depend on being fed by hand, the bond of trust that hand feeding establishes between bird and human being will persist perhaps throughout the bird's entire life. Photo by Louise Van der Meid.

Index